WORLD
of
WONDER

Rhulani Mathebula

Copyright © 2019 Rhulani Mathebula

All rights reserved.

No part of this book may be reproduced in any manner, mechanically or electronically, including tape or other audio recordings and photocopying, without the written permission of the author, except for reasonable excerpts for research and reviewing purposes.

First Edition, 2019
ISBN: 978-1-77605-599-9

Layout & Typesetting
Janet Von Kleist

Published by Kwarts Publishers
www.kwartspublishers.co.za

Dedication

I dedicate this book to all the men and women in my circle through whom some of these poems were born:

My son, Lulama, who is my inspiration for excellence, and Mpilehle, my sleeping son who lives on in my heart and forever with Papa – we shall meet again.

My legend of a father, and my king, Mr Makasani Daniel Mathebula: you are brave and bold, and I still learn from you.

The queen of my heart, my mother, Mrs Mavila Rebecca Mathebula: you nurtured your nature into me.

My sisters and brothers: I am because you are.

My friends: you hold a special place in my heart.

My spiritual parents, the Beloved David and Prophetess Prudence Msiza: He gave me 'you' after His own heart, and if it weren't for Rev E.G. Seleka and Rev (Mama) R.M. Seleka, I would not know quality.

My Hallelujah belongs to You, God, my Father, my Anchor, my Strength, my Pillar, my Healer, my Peace, my Joy; my All. The giver of life, the giver of gifts. You keep calling me to a higher dimension – I heed, oh God, I heed.

About the book

World of Wonder is written by the remarkable Rhulani Mathebula, author of *Art of the Heart*. *World of Wonder* was born from the very nature of the world – a wondrous place to live in with its uncertainties, ups and downs, bliss, turmoil, hope, and all the amazing things that await us. The book takes you on a journey of emotions, and it quickens deep thinking. It takes you to a world of imagination and wonder. It tickles your funny bone, and yes, it makes you realise that you are not insane when you feel the way you sometimes do. Go ahead, create your own stories and dine in these words – enjoy.

Contents

He lies	13
Loss	14
My identity	15
Brothers standing side by side	16
You lived	17
Limitations of money	18
The woman	19
Sorrow	21
Ugly duckling	22
Counting blessings and misfortunes	23
And there was peace	24
Cricket – the game	25
Year-end 2017	26
The power of words	27
Vultures	28
Caged	29
Gold inside of me	30
Thank you	31
My children	32
Late	33
I'm colourful	35
It was me	36
Just to hear it	37
The breaking point	38

I loved her	39
How are you?	40
Bit bait	42
There is more	43
In love	44
Who is the most beautiful?	46
Listen, feel	47
Love my decision	48
Two to tango	49
My hands	50
The blind spot	51
They meet, they greet, they part	52
Diamond	53
Admiring my freckles	54
I'm going to roll them away	55
I love you – I love you too	56
Sign language	57
Foundation	58
Shifted my focus	59
Caught between two fires	60
I am doing well	61
The girl, the woman	63
Talent perfected	65
Weeds	66
Attention	67
My life – the story	68
We are family	69
The wonder in praise	70
Indicators	72
Tigress	73

WORLD
of
WONDER

Rhulani Mathebula

He lies

he said I would not amount to anything – he lied
he said I would never recover – he lied
he said I would die before I step into my house – he lied
he said I would die before my book is published – he lied
he said I was not good enough – he lied
he said I am ugly – he lied
Did God not say, "It is very good,"
after creating his masterpiece?

he said I was not worthy of stepping into the holiest – he lied
Was not the curtain torn from top to bottom?
Did He not die and also rise for me?
he lies about anything and everything
When he lies, he speaks his native language;
he speaks from his resources
No wonder it sounds true – though not
he masters the art of accusing the
brethren – condemning them
But was it not erased, the handwriting that stood against us?
And is there yet condemnation for them that are in Christ?
Do not believe him, he lies
¹Ni vula sathani wa hemba

---

1   The devil – he lies

Loss

I never knew just how deep the pain of loss goes
The void, the emptiness
And the constant reminders everywhere
The longing to cuddle him once more, or
twice more, or a lifetime more
Maybe to look at his big eyes
To hear him cry and to change his nappy

And the wonder of what he would be and how life would be
And the desire to somehow wake up from this nightmare
And I stand to salute all who've lost
A husband or a wife,
A mother or a father,
A friend, a sister or a brother
A son or a daughter
You are strong

My identity

I am the image of the Creator
I am an ambassador
I am more than a conqueror
I am a branch on the Vine
I am the redeemed
I am a friend of God
I am an heir
I am above, not beneath; head not tail
I am sited with Him in the heavenly realms
I am loved to love, blessed to bless
Healed to heal, saved to save
I am sealed by the Holy Spirit
I am more than can be seen
I am His
Yes! I am the son of THE I AM THAT I AM

BROTHERS STANDING SIDE BY SIDE

And if you spied from a distance, you would think
they were giving a speech at some inauguration
Well dressed and well kept
From a distance, you would not see the pain they hid so well
Perhaps that explains why they stood side by side
So that when one is weak, the other may pick him up
Brothers stood side by side like lions roaring for their pride
To bid farewell to their sleeping sister – my aunt
My dad and uncle stood side by side

You Lived

Earth has a record of your birth and death
Though just for five weeks you made a quick trip to earth
And to your Maker, you returned
I would have loved to keep you to hear you say "mama"
Though you never left the hospital, your
footprints are along the path I walk
Places to which we travelled together while I carried you

Your fingerprints are deep in my heart
And I still wonder how a tiny being could have
such an impact in the world so wide
And how such short moments cannot be forgotten
And why you left in such a hurry
The bond between a mother and a child; my child, my son
I have you memorised – I had great plans for us
And wherever I go, I wonder what you would do there

I still cry for you – I remember you, and I still
imagine how life would be like with you
You have irreplaceable value, my son
I held you, I looked into your eyes, I
saw you smile, I heard you cry
I will cherish that
And carry the hope to see you again
You lived, and left and left huge footprints in my heart
I remember you

Rhulani Mathebula

LIMITATIONS OF MONEY

Does not prevent heartache, neither does it heal
Does not save a life neither, does it wake the dead
Does not buy health
Does not buy a friend or a child
Does not make one wise
Etcetera . . .

The woman

So, what makes her a woman?
Is it the diamond on her finger?
The pearls
The sweet fragrance she wears
Or her lipstick?
Is it her cat-like walk?
Or natural sweet talk?

What makes her a woman?
It is her image as God predestined
It is her virtue
She sees a need, and she meets it
In her heart lives compassion; she defends the tender
And forgives the offender
She is both gorgeous and courageous
Even in defeat, she finds her feet
No matter the circumstances – she gets
up, dresses up and shows up
She is queen, not necessarily married
to a king, but born queen
She fixes other queen's crowns with
no fear of being dethroned

She is wise like an ant gathering for winter in summer
She is bold like an eagle facing the storm head-on
She is a brave lioness – roars less, but catches her prey
Like a chameleon, she wears many colours
Like a bee, she stings when it matters most, and if
you have been stung by a woman, you can attest
She is gold put into a fire: tested, tried and can be trusted
She is daring and caring
She is bold, she is gold
And does not wait until told, or old
To release her influence

Sorrow

Sorrow burrowed deep into my heart
Sorrow hallowed my heart
Uninvited it made room for itself
What words express the depth or the width thereof?
With what can I liken it?

It's like a thorn that cannot be removed; a
thorn to die, rot and be felt no more
And we ever ask: "Why me?"
And at times when I think the thorn died – I feel it again
Nonetheless, we know that brethren
everywhere know the affliction
Was I to know it before I did
I would have burrowed myself in a cave,
hibernating until my Maker comes for me
Perhaps that explains why I never knew
before I knew just how deep it goes

Ugly duckling

The odd one out
My father is the king lion, my mother
the lioness, my siblings the cubs
But I am the leopard – I'm spotted and easily spotted
My father's roar has pruned the cubs
My mother's care kept them well-rounded
But the leopard kept climbing trees, as is its nature
As though not natured in the lion family (me)

Counting blessings and misfortunes

From dawn to dusk, I counted my blessings and lost count
Then sat to count my misfortunes; one,
two, then scratched my head
No need to scale them; the writing is on the wall
Clear as day I am blessed, not cursed
I have much to be grateful for
Loved beyond measure; esteemed high by my Maker
Shall I give You glory or honour for all of these
and more You deserve – my Blesser
I love You, yet You first loved me with such
love to which nothing compares
I shall often sit to count my blessings
For bliss is born in me when I come
to realise how blessed I am

AND THERE WAS PEACE

The calm, still, sweet breeze . . . hmmm, peace at last
And I can breathe without choking
After the storm that blinded me
That deafened me
That seemed to move me from my standing
That had me questioning my very existence
Peace at last

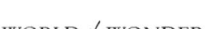

CRICKET – THE GAME

You can either spectate, play or retire
It is easier to pick the faults of the players when spectating
I have played, spectated, retired and I am playing again
I played ball many times

One time while playing ball
The batsman hit a six – a call for
celebration for those in his team
But for me, it was game over out of the field
Before I landed, another ball was soon in
I looked and felt pity for her – smooth
and never played before
It had better be a four
That way, she shall remain in the game
Or even better: a catch to send the batsman packing
Who knows? Perhaps the bowler's hands are a better place

Year-end 2017

So, the year has come to an end
A time to send one's mind to the beginning
To count losses and gains
To wish things had worked out differently
and to accept that they did not
To hope for a better 2018

Though we know not for sure what is to come, we
can be sure we will stand if we stand side by side
To lend a helping hand to those hardest hit
To bend and lift a brother up
To share a joke or a smile
A meal or walk with them a mile
To heal and mend broken ties
To stand together as one
To keep this brand soaring
Shaping the brand-new you for the brand-new year

The power of words

Words persuade, convince, strengthen,
give life – the list is endless
Words can dampen one's spirit, destroy a dream
Words, once planted grow and bear fruit after their kind
Be sure to sow kind ones to reap kindness
Do not underestimate their power to alter your
course because the power is in your very tongue
So, put them to good use
Do not misuse the power – the power in you
And if you put them in the right order,
you can order anything

Vultures

Birds of prey, pray they do not prey on you
Opportunistic be not their opportunity
With keen vision, they watch their prey from afar
Patiently awaiting a sign of weakness, they land
in pairs, and they will not spare anyone
With strong, curved beaks for tearing flesh, soft
organs like the heart are in grave danger
They carry prey with their strong legs,
they carry prey through the air
And if the punishing wind does not finish you
They drop you to your doom

Caged

Caged like a bird wishing to fly
Like a wild donkey wishing to go wild
Self-caged in a wall-less cage
Caged by fear of the unknown
Caged by fear of "what shall they think or say"
Stretch your hands
There are no walls
Run wild
Run free
Fly high
Fly very high
See the caged around you also take flight

Gold inside of me

A wealth of minerals: undug, buried, hidden
The finest treasure lives within me
I shall keep digging
Until I discover the abundant wealth buried inside of me
The deposits the Maker has planted in me
And when I do, I shall work it – multiply
it to my own and other's profit
Great gains await me – await us inside of me
So help me, destroy not our wealth

THANK YOU

My sincere gratitude to You, faithful I Am that I Am
Thank You, for you saw my substance, yet unformed
Thank You for wisdom and understanding
Thank You for peace and calm
Thank You for the thanks I am yet to give
Hallelujah!

My children

I conceived you
Before I met your father
I carried you in my spirit
And it made no difference that you were
yet to be – for you already were
And so for you, I give thanks

LATE

Woken up by the sunlight piercing through the
window curtain. Not as usual by the alarm.
An adrenaline rush sends me flying out of
my bed with no time to make it up.
My toothbrush in front of me I cannot find, then finding
my old one, I brush my teeth and do what seems like
bathing, focusing only on the essentials while shouting at
my son to do what I know he does not do: "Hurry up".

My temper rockets sky high and I am no different
to him who is high save for his calm.
And the car keys, hidden in plain sight;
the plight of being late.
Once found, my multitasking is at play:
hair, makeup and driving.
Passing the amber light which I normally do not.
And sneering at the 60km/hr driver before
me who is well on time. "Driiiiive!"
As though her car is standing still.
Sadly, in all this, I am still late.

Worse, I didn't see how beautiful I am.
I didn't see my colleague who needed
a ride just to get to work.
I didn't see how blessed I am to see the sunlight.
I didn't smell the morning's breeze.
I did not see the wonderful surroundings I smile at usually
I even forgot to say: "Thank You, Lord, for another
beautiful day" so much I miss when I am late.

Rhulani Mathebula

So, I promised myself to be always on time
to avoid such cases that often occur when late.
And if by chance I miss it, I promise to keep
my cool for when in a hurry, I worry.
Yet, if at a certain age, you have not climbed
society's ladder, you are also deemed "late".

Late to start over
Late to try again
Late for the promotion
Late to have kids
Late to be married
Late to buy a car or a house
Late to . . .

Sadly, there is much that one miss when the society's time tick
Then I promised myself once again that
my time is best when it is my time

I'm colourful

I'm careful, sometimes I'm careless
I play and dance, but sometimes I sit and laze around
I'm brilliant, but sometimes I do things so stupid
you'll wonder where I hid my brilliance
I'm fair, but sometimes very unfair and my
son says it well: "Mama, you are unfair"
I laugh; I laugh hard, but sometimes I'm angry
I'm bold, but sometimes I'm afraid
I'm a happy soul, but sometimes I'm sad
I'm an adult, but sometimes I'm childish
I'm beautiful, but I can be ugly, very ugly
I'm crazy
I'm funny
I'm fun
I am strong in my weakness
Oh, beautiful colours of me
I'm colourful

Rhulani Matjhebula

It was me

It was my fault by default
I let things in my life
I watched them steal my peace
In fear of watching them leave, I suffered in silence
I was not blind
I saw it
I saw it all
I let them dance on my precious head
They just love to dance on heads that avail themselves

I blamed them, saying they were mean
I said they were cruel, greedy, selfish, you name it
No, I let them
Well, enough
No more. Not on my head. No, no, nooo
Only I wish I could go back to every event where I
let things dance on my head before I became me
I would have the pleasure to look them in
the eye and tell them where to get off
Or even better: cause them to fall while
they enjoyed dancing on my head

Just to hear it

Stay and say it
Say it once, twice, countless times
Say it. Say it like you mean it. Say "I love you"

I sacrificed myself just to hear it
And I, I suffered just to hear it
Well, enough. I'll say it to myself
"I love you, I love you, I love you, Rhulani"
I love you truly, I love you deeply, and won't let things
hurt you just so you can hear a phoney "I love you"
I love you, I do
Not in a selfish manner
But I love you so much so that I can
love others this much too

The breaking point

The climax, the tipping point, the point of no return
I was there and woke up on the other side
and boy it is a place of green pastures
Where streams of still waters flow
And the land overflows with milk and honey
Here the tables are spread, prepared for me, and they can
only watch when I dine at the table fashioned for me

Thank you. How could I have fallen to the
other side if it had not been for you?
Thank you. You've done your job, and you've
done it well – a gold medal I award you
You've burned this gold to perfection
I pray that the things that are burning you
burn you to the breaking point
So that you, like me, will offer them a gold medal
Having woken up on the other side
The breaking point, a point of surrender

I loved her

She died in a car accident
We met just three times, but her kind-
hearted soul so gentle drew me to her
A few words, a few giggles, and a few
smiles our paths crossed
Her deep, coarse voice I still hear
Then she left – to a world unknown to me
And I cried – not only because she left, but
also because I did not tell her I loved her
Too precious, too short her life

Had I known that day we took a stroll that
it was the last together on this planet
I would have walked further
I was wrong
I said: "We would meet again"
Maybe not too wrong, just not on this planet
And to all I love – I love you today
In case I never get to say on this planet earth "I love you"

How are you?

Almost a cliché: "How are you?"
We hear it 100 times a day and say the same
And every time we say: "I'm fine, how are you"
and proceed with our hectic lives
Fixing things that keep breaking and
breaking things that are fixed
The vanity of life
How are you?
Whoever says I'm hollowed; I'm hurting
I'm struggling
I'm dwindling
I'm breaking
I'm ashamed
I'm bitter
I'm lonely
I'm drowning
I'm weak
At least we say "I'm physically sick" because
anything deep we keep to ourselves

Surely, no one hangs her laundry dirty
Tell a confidant; hang the laundry
But not yourself, my friend
Don't hang yourself
How are you, my friend?
My sister
My brother
My son
I will not judge

What have you done; what have they
done to you? How are you?
How is life treating you now?
Are you carrying a load you cannot bear?
I know a friend, my friend who sticks closer than a brother
No deed is too deep – It is not too bad, you can be repaired
Let me take you to Him

They took me to Him, and He rescued me
How are you?

Bit bait

I am my Father's goldfish
He feeds me
He loves me
He supplies from his abundance
I pray: "Daddy, I need a worm"
And He said: "You cannot stomach it yet, wait a bit"
I waited and waited: "Daddy, my worm"
In the ocean so vast I saw others like me get their worm
I went back to Him to ask in despair: "Daddy, my worm!"
And again, He said: "Wait a bit my precious goldfish"

And I started looking at myself . . .
Maybe I'm too gold?
Maybe I've wronged Daddy too many times?
Maybe I swam the wrong way?
Maybe, maybe, maybe, maybe . . .

While in deep thoughts, a worm finer than
I could ever imagine swam my way
Oh, Daddy! Thank you!
I went for it with my mouth open wide
But the hook caught me, and it pulled
me out of the water to die
But, as always, Daddy came to my rescue
He nurtured my wound
But I'm scared, again, and keep biting into the bait
Enough! No more bait!
I can smell the bait . . .

THERE IS MORE

What I have is not all I'll have
What I have seen is not all there is to see
What I have heard is not all there is to hear
What I have experienced is not all there is to experience
What I have done is not all I can do
What I am is not all that I will be

I want more than I have seen
More than I have heard
More than I have imagined
So, I'm diving deep into myself to find more

In love

I had a strange feeling
The type I feel when in love
It was so strange for I was as single as they
come – not even potential nearby
But I was deep in love
The butterflies
The naughty eyes
The glow
What is this, who am I in love with so deep?
While in this ecstasy, I took another look at myself
How beautiful I am
I looked deeper to see the same beauty
if not mere inside of me
I saw how strong I have become, how
competent, how confident, how beautiful
Look what the rain and the snow brought forth, the
sprouts; Oh God, Oh God, Oh God, Oh God!

I have fallen for me
I love this woman, I'm in love with her
For the first time, I see deep inside of her
I cannot believe how much I have missed
I love this woman with love so deep, so strong
I love her highs, I love her lows
I love her weakness by which she
becomes humble and strong
I love her deeply
I love her truly
I love her dearly
I love her passion to love, to believe,
to live despite . . . despite it all
I'm in love with me, and this love compels
me to love my neighbour as myself

Who is the most beautiful?

It caused consuming jealousy for the queen envying
snow-white while she, despite her age, was so fair
Should beauty be compared?
I leave it to you to answer
But my take is all are beautiful
All are unique
And each is the most beautiful compared to self
And deep within each is more beauty than can be seen
So, you are in trouble if you try to select the most beautiful
But if you are searching for your kind of beautiful
Search deep, search very deep because the beauty is untold
Sadly, we're enculturated to seek and
see the beauty with our eyes
Wisdom sees true beauty
Close your eyes and see the beauty
Feel the beauty
Hear the beauty . . . even in silence

LISTEN, FEEL

Feel the morning breeze, hear the birds sing
Feel the rays of the sun, listen to the silence of the moon
Listen to a child's first cry, feel the joy of his bearer
Listen to the dog's night bark, feel the echo
Listen to the pain of loss and the joy of gain
Listen to the growling hunger that fuels the lion's hunt

Feel her heartbeat; feel without touching
Feel the brokenness, the sadness of the woman smiling
Feel the joy and passion that drives a young man
Listen and feel the morning breeze
that gently brushes your ears
Wiping yesterday's tears
Close your ears
Listen, feel

LOVE MY DECISION

"Love is a decision," they taught me
A lesson I refused to learn
It takes feeling to take action
And a sober mind to make a decision
Sadly, in both cases, a decision has been made
Yes, in feeling by default and indeed
the consequences my fault
Still, I cried foul
So deep I loved
So true, but why?

"Love is a decision" a lesson I refused to learn
Yet I'm an intellectual, brilliant and excellent
But in deciding who or what to love for too long a time
I remained immature (unformed, unripe, young)
Refusing to learn
After so many weepings I now know to
think with my head, not heart

Two to Tango

Tango – what a dance
Can I term it the love dance?
For two only can dance just two
Any more – no tango
Any less – no tango
Two, together, dazzling on the dance floor
Applaud by spectators
Yet the two hear them not, deep in the dance
side to side – graceful and beautiful

My hands

They said they were wrinkled
They were right; that's what they saw
But I see the fine art of my Maker decorating the fine lines
They said they were missing a ring on the left hand
They were right; that's what they saw
But I see the bride of Christ; beautiful and wonderful
These hands – they touch to heal
They touch and turn to gold everything they hold
They make, they take (receive), they give
They keep, they protect, they love, they
nurture – that's their nature
They make good what they find to do

The blind spot

Warned of it in K53 – a dangerous spot
And was made to repeat "mirror, mirror, blind spot"
Not merely in words, but in action – an
important part of the journey
Keeping at it "mirror, mirror, blind spot"
To spot the unspotted parts of my journey
The parts undetected by my mirrors (the grey areas)
Dangerous areas to keep check, especially
when a decision is to be taken
To change lanes, to accelerate, or to brake whatever
wise decision to ensure my and other's safety

Oh, how I mistook this lesson for a driving lesson only
Whereas it is a life lesson missing the
blind spot of my journey
And crushing into my and other's detriment
Kaboom! Kaboom! Kaboom!
Over and over again
I thank God for healing and restoration
For redemption
For shining His light on the blind spot
I spot it spot on
The blind spot

Rhulani Mathebula

They meet, they greet, they part

Like oil and water, they do not mix
Yet this is both water – salt water
Indian and Atlantic oceans: they meet, they greet, they part
They do not mix or cross
Whose hand did this?
This hand must be mightier that I can think
Or rather: whose Word did this?
This Word must be mightier than I can imagine

They meet, they greet, they part as instructed
They are not distracted
Not by my wonder or marvel
Nothing I say or do destructs their course
They meet, they greet, they part
As swiftly and quickly as they should
There are people I must meet and
with their amazing souls part
After imparting a part of me
And them their part to me
While others I must mingle with for life
Like the sea and the seashore
Lord help me . . .

Diamond

Only a diamond cuts a diamond
Causing its sparkle (to come out) and it is fulfilled
what was said "an iron sharpens another"
And this diamond laid dormant, unpolished, covered by dust
Yet she was still a diamond
Never taking the shape of dust though camouflaged as such
And when her season was due, they
(the diamonds) shaped her
And it is fulfilled what was said, ". . . so
shall man pour upon your bosom"
My gratitude to diamonds that shaped and sharpened me
Every now and then do it again, lest I gather
dust and rust and sparkle no more
I shall as you did cut, shape and sharpen other diamonds
And when they sparkle more than I, I shall rejoice

Admiring My Freckles

They teased me about it: they said it was ugly
For lack of wisdom, I agreed, wishing them away
But they stayed – my package
I concealed them, but never completely
They would spring up and face me
They would stare at me in the mirror
"We aren't going anywhere"

It's as if He stood at a distance
marvelling at me (His creation)
And from that distance, He splashed them,
and they doted my whole body
His finishing touches
And He smiled: "It is good", and I concur
thinking, Oh God, I'll beat this drum
It is beautiful
It is colourful
It is wonderful
Perfect
Admirable
Adorable
The wonder of God's creation
Hmm, what words shall I use to express the admiration?

I'M GOING TO ROLL THEM AWAY

My feelings, will roll them away – if not two way
No matter how true I feel, how deep, how strong I love
If the same is not returned, I'll roll, I'll roll it away

For if I keep it, it shall eat me alive
It shall drain the beauty inside of me
Eroding to the core myself
What's in it for me?
The applause of those who watch from a distance?

No, I cannot keep it – I'll roll it away
Into the rubbish bin
They take it away to the landfill; they'll burn it to ashes
If it refuses to die, it will grow far away from me

I love you – I love you too

Misused words
Anybody can say "I love you – I love you too"
How I wish for a barricade to barricade the words
Prevent them from being said, unless they are true
I swallowed my wish for it shall never come true
They'll keep saying it just to say it
I cried for me; I cried, for I love to hear these words
For a long time, I was hypnotised by the
sound of them – just words (empty)
Awakening a Hallelujah
I learned to pair the words with the actions
Frankly, I would rather see them than hear them
for they are very (and I repeat) very obvious
I close my ears and open my big eyes and
watch to see clearly love in action

Sign language

An official language in my country of birth
I can only say thank you in this language
Yet I have spoken it so many times
Without any formal teaching
And expected the hearer to decode the coded
message hidden in my sign language

And I cried foul when the hearer could not
decode the hidden meaning in my signals
Rhulani
You were wrong to create a language and not explain it
Shakespeare had an explanatory note, lest
the reader wouldn't understand
What shall we call it, the language you spoke?
We cannot call it sign language for sign
language can be understood
Let's rather call it mystery language

We rejoice for you chose to forsake that language
Open your mouth and let it be known
what's in your heart and mind
Shuuuuu liberty

Foundation

All structures have it
Not a "may" a "must" in the building process
A fundamental stage cannot be bypassed
Any fault weakness spoils the design and the beauty
Over time the winds and storms will test the foundation
Cracks, and ultimately the crumble,
will testify of the foundation
They will say whether it is rock or sand
Each builder ought to choose to either build on rock or sand
For both times will tell

I met a friend, and we built our own
house on fantasies and fallacies
In fact, frankly, we started in the air, enjoying
what seemed to be a beautiful building
Any stranger looking from a distance would
say: "Oh, what a beautiful building!
Wishing to have one just like that"
Shame, it was only a matter of time before
the winds tested the foundation
And there was none – our building collapsed to rise no more
Oh, my friend, I shall start at the bottom in future
I hope for your sake you've learned your lesson . . .

SHIFTED MY FOCUS

There's a spot, a big brown ugly spot
Like a blemish on my skin
So obvious to any who has eyes
I kept staring at it, trying to get rid of it with all my might
Yet it stayed, it seemed the more I tried to
remove it, the more visible it became

I wondered what I ever did to deserve this spot
And I cried why, when, how?
This is too much
How do I carry this spot with me every day without
knowing if, or when, it will ever go away?

This spot on me, I hate
One last time I shifted my focus and saw the rest of me
Oh boy, is it beautiful!
And my heart was overflowing with gladness and gratitude
I shined and polished the rest of me, but
some days I would see the spot
It looked faint; it seemed to get fainter and
fainter with less attention given to it

I continued in search of what I am
I am more than my spot
Oh, what beauty I failed to see while focusing on a spot
It was still there – it did not matter much
The Lord, my God, disarmed its grip – its hold over me
And before I knew it, it was gone
And it came to pass what was said: "Seek ye first the
kingdom of God and all these things shall be added unto you"

Caught between two fires

A young man caught between two strong fires
Why they compete, I don't know
Consuming this champ caught between them
How does he choose between the fire that raised him?
The fire that fed him, protected him
The fire that kept him warm in cold
nights and made him who he is
And the fire of his own heart a part of him
The fire that now keeps him warm
How does he choose?
Can anyone help him choose?

And he bows down in utter anguish, for
he knows he cannot choose
He needs both the fires to burn
To burn for him, and to burn together
How beautiful that fire would be if only
they could learn to burn together

I am doing well

Despite myself, despite it all, I am doing well
On my own running a household and lights
are always on (save for load shedding)
I am father; I am mother
I am bold; I am beautiful
I am doing well

There is no disadvantage for me
For even when it seems I am losing, I am winning
I am doing well

Through every detour, every bad break, every turmoil
Every station I stood
Rising from every fall
And the repercussion of every bad decision
And showing up despite it all

Through thick, through thin, you are standing
And your smile, my God, your smile never fading
Despite it all, you still share your joy
and your accrued wisdom
You are doing well

A tap on the shoulder, Rhuli
A standing ovation for you
Behind every strong woman, there is a Man (Father)
He holds her
He keeps her
He heals her
He leads her

He strengthens her
She can do all things through Him
(Christ) who strengthens her
Hallelujah!

The girl, the woman

I still see her in a floral dress
No shoes on
Chasing butterflies
And her father sits watching her
She feels safe, she feels loved
No care in the world and when she catches
one, she runs to sit on his lap
"Papa, look what I found"
I still see his smile
A father's love so deep
"Well done my princess, well done"

And she looks at him and says: Papa I feel
You feel
I feel your and mama's kisses on my body
He could not comprehend it
And if she could show it; the collage of kisses
They would look amazing
Only mama's kisses show
For papa does not wear lipstick
Still, his kisses stick

And to her love, she says, "I feel your
kisses all over my body"
I chase not butterflies, but a carrier
Still, with you, I feel safe

And if I were to show a collage of your
kisses, they would look amazing
Like papa's they do not show for you
too do not wear lipstick
But they are there, and I feel them
The girl, the woman; your woman my love

Talent perfected

From the Philippines, Charice, a young girl sang
She sang a song by the talented Celine Dion
And reached those ridiculously high notes
And I listened, taking notes
Talent perfected

I cannot sing, but what I can do, I do
I have a rather course voice for speaking, not singing
And learned hands
So, I took on writing
Sharpening and multiplying the talent given me
Causing it to shine so the world could dine
Dine on the talent worked on the talent perfected

And we love it, we do
We shake our heads
And cover our open mouth with our hands
Some even place their hands on their heads
In moments that take their breath away
Moments presented by those who
perfected the talent given them
We all have it: a gift, a talent
So, make the time to perfect yours
There's room for all of us

Weeds

Weeds sprout like the seeds I planted in my garden
Just as green, and from a distance just
as beautiful – well camouflaged
Bearing after their own kind, the weeds
spread to take over my garden
But what shall I do with them?
For they are neither edible nor beautiful in close range

So, I took the time to pluck them out
one by one from the root
And when I bent over, I saw more weeds
in my garden than in my neighbour's
Ah, how beautiful and full of good greens my garden is
I shall keep plucking them out
For when one looks away, they grow again

ATTENTION

Women love it
Not only us
Everything loves attention
Garden, dishes, houses, children, friends . . .

And when deprived of it
The cracks start to show
Overgrown, ugly gardens
Foul odour in kitchens,
Spiders and cracks in houses

And to my man: if you deny me your attention
The cracks you cause will grow so big
you'll fall right through them
Never to return

My life – the story

I view my life like a story
Pages and chapters read are history
Each year is a chapter, each day a page
As I gracefully age

Some pages cause me to share a tear
Such pages I wish to tear
Some pages and chapters I would repeat if I could
But there is no going back I continue as I should

Discovering mysteries in each page
Growing at each stage
Becoming older, wiser and stronger
I am an infant no longer

I impact better the characters with whom I interact
Having learnd to respond rather than to react
I will keep reading until the end
In complete reliance to the Author – Alpha
and Omega beginning and the end

We are family

They define family
They say, "It is a group consisting of
parents and their children"
I say, "Family is who you love and who loves you"
We are deeper than DNA, lineage, culture or colour

We are tied together by cords of love
Love running through our veins like blood
The very essence of life
We all have a place in our hearts that needs filling
A longing for belonging

Family is that component
To stand together against any opponent such as
sickness, failure, loss, fear, disappointment . . .
That component to complement achievement
With whom to share a smile, a joke, laughter, wealth . . .

So let us unite and ignite
The fire within us
Together we are a formidable force
Walking side by side throughout life's course

The wonder in praise

I have found my place
I'm set ablaze
When I praise
When I gaze at the One
His beauty
His excellence
He is Almighty

His Spirit without measure
Lifts away all pressure
Pressure buried in my soul
And my soul sings a song
And groans words I cannot utter
Worry melts away like butter

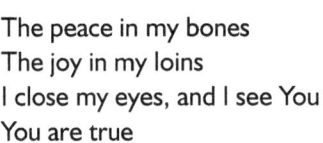

The peace in my bones
The joy in my loins
I close my eyes, and I see You
You are true

And lift my hands in surrender
Filled with the wonder
Of His Greatness
His awesomeness
His Holiness
Oh, gracious Father
There is only You, there is no other

Of all the things I have seen, felt, heard, and touched, the best is in your presence
Yet I cannot fully explain it

Indicators

Vehicles are equipped with signals to speak to other drivers
Hazards signalling danger
Indicators to turn right or left
These signals support the decisions of the other

So, my friend, do not dictate
Or spectate in our journey
Indicate, communicate

I took too late to see
The hazards you displayed

So I'm indicating
Communicating
I'm saying that I'm turning the opposite
direction and we are drifting apart
Can you hear me?

TIGRESS

Black stripes on her brown coat
White patches can be seen especially on her face
Just as charming as the domestic cat
But this cat's senses and claws are sharper

The love she holds in her heart is too deep
And she cannot in the same heart hold hate
She is scarred in won battles
She is scared no more

She nurtures her young and releases them to their destiny
She will pounce any mate presenting a threat to her young

www.ingramcontent.com/pod-product-compliance
Lightning Source LLC
Chambersburg PA
CBHW031310060426
42444CB00033B/1153